# Valentine Crafts

# Valentine Crafts

★ A Holiday Craft Book ★

★ Judith Hoffman Corwin ★

**FRANKLIN WATTS**

New York ★ Chicago ★ London ★ Toronto ★ Sydney

★ **Also by Judith Hoffman Corwin** ★

**African Crafts**
**Asian Crafts**
**Latin American and Caribbean Crafts**

**Colonial American Crafts: The Home**
**Colonial American Crafts: The School**
**Colonial American Crafts: The Village**

**Easter Crafts**
**Halloween Crafts**

**Papercrafts**

*Forthcoming Books*

**Christmas Crafts**
**Hanukkah Crafts**
**Kwanzaa Crafts**
**Thanksgiving Crafts**

★ **For Jules Arthur and Oliver Jamie** ★

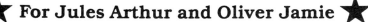

Library of Congress Cataloging-in-Publication Data

Corwin, Judith Hoffman.
  Valentine crafts / Judith Hoffman Corwin.
    p.     cm.—(Holiday crafts)
  Includes bibliographical references (p.     ) and index.
  ISBN 0-531-11146-6
    1. Valentine decorations—Juvenile literature.    2. Handicraft—Juvenile
literature.    3. Valentine cookery—Juvenile literature.    [1. Valentine
decorations.    2. Handicraft.    3. Cookery.]    I. Title.    II. Series: Corwin,
Judith Hoffman. Holiday Crafts.
  TT900.V34C66      1994
  745.594′1—dc20              93-11970  CIP  AC

# Contents

# About Valentine's Day

Valentine's Day is such a fun-filled holiday. Valentines are either made or bought. They are exchanged and collected, to be saved for years. There are heart-shaped boxes of chocolates, flowers, and special greeting cards and maybe a secret admirer. And delicious things to eat. The custom of Valentine's Day has traveled through the ages, from very early beginnings.

There are many legends about how Valentine's Day got its name long ago, but nobody knows exactly why we celebrate Valentine's Day or when it started. Some scholars think that Valentine's Day was originally the Lupercalia, a joyous Roman feast for lovers that was celebrated around what is now February 14 on our calendar. When the Romans became Christians, the Lupercalia was replaced by a holiday in honor of St. Valentine, a Christian martyr. St. Valentine, who died more than 1,700 years ago, is now popularly considered to be the patron saint of lovers. And St. Valentine's Day has become the time to tell people you like them by sending greetings—called, of course, "valentines."

People still enjoy making their own greetings, even though valentines have been manufactured in the United States for more than 100 years. Examples of early handmade valentines—with fold-outs, satin ribbons, lace, and hearts—can still be found. You will be able to create your own valentines by making some of the projects in this book. Someday they may be treasured antiques!

# Let's Get Started

This book will help you find out about the Valentine's Day holiday, its legends and history. It is full of ideas for making greeting cards, decorations, gift wrappings, presents, and wonderful treats to eat. Often you will be able to make everything yourself, from everyday household supplies and objects. Use your imagination and you will be surprised at what you can create. The treasures you make will add color and excitement to your celebration.

Directions for some of the projects include patterns for you to use to make a copy of what is shown. You don't want to cut up this book, so copy the pattern with tracing paper. Begin by placing a piece of tracing paper over the pattern in the book. Using a pencil with a soft lead, trace the outline of the pattern. Turn the paper over and rub all over the pattern with the pencil. Turn it over again, and tape or hold it down carefully on the paper or fabric you have chosen to work with. Draw over your original lines, pressing hard on the pencil. Lift the tracing-paper pattern and you are ready to go on with the other instructions for your project.★

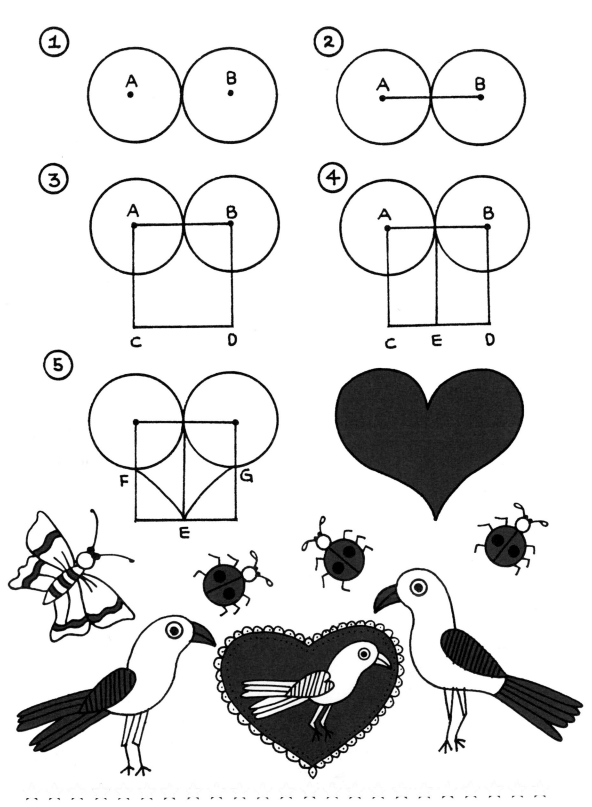

# Hearts Galore!

Hearts are the most popular symbol for love and, therefore, for Valentine's Day. Here's an easy way to draw a very nice heart, using a compass. Just follow the simple illustrations and you will have a perfect heart all ready to decorate. On this and the following pages there are lots of great-looking designs you can use with your compass-drawn heart. Sometimes the heart is decorated inside and out, and other times it is given a central position in the design. All you need is a compass with a pencil, a piece of paper, and colored felt-tip markers or colored pencils. Try using these designs to make cards, wrapping paper, bookmarks, and room decorations, then cut out a perfect heart.

**HERE'S HOW TO DO IT**★

**HEART DRAWN WITH A COMPASS**★

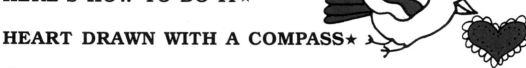

**1.** Draw two circles, the same size, and have them touch, as shown in the illustration.

**2.** Now draw a line from the center of each circle, connecting point A to point B.

**3.** Check the illustration and draw a square, connecting points A, B, C, and D.

**4.** Draw a line down the middle of the square to point E, as shown.

**5.** Now draw a curved line, as shown in the illustration, from point E to F on one side of the heart, and from point E to G on the other side. You can use this method to draw any size heart—just change the size of the circles that you start with.

## CUT OUT A PERFECT HEART ★

Using a piece of paper and scissors, you can quickly cut out a perfect heart. You can also make a simple heart by folding a piece of paper in half and cutting out a heart, as shown in the illustration. First draw the shape onto the paper with a pencil. Then cut on that line, using it as a guide. ★

## OLD-FASHIONED CUT-OUT HEARTS★

Now you're ready to make a folded and cut-out valentine. This one is similar to some that were made over a hundred years ago. A circle is decorated with large and small cut-out hearts.

 With a pencil, trace the outline of a plate on a piece of paper. Cut out the circle. Fold it in half, and then in half again, and then in half again, as shown. Checking the illustration, draw hearts onto the folded paper and carefully cut them out. Open up your circle and all sixteen hearts will appear. If you want to, you can write a message on your cut-out valentine or decorate it by going around the outlines of the hearts with colored markers.★

One of the earliest drawings of St. Valentine, from a book printed in the late 15th century.

Valentinus

concili zu Antiochia mit aller deßmals gege
auß vrteil Gregorij des Cesariensischen bisch
was vnd nachfolgend vmb cristenlichs gl
Manes 8 ketzer auß Persia pirtig ein listi
lebens ist zu disen zeiten gewesen. Di
fordert. rij. iunger zu ime mit den er in alle di
vnd er machet zu ertödtung der betrognen
re von kirchpruchigen vnd ertrachten lüger
folger betroge. dañ er sprach das Christus d
haftigen leichnam sunder ein eytle pildnus e
ketzer mit seinen nachfolgern sprach das zw
der des bösen. einer des liechts. der ander de
ment vnd sahe allain das new an. Also hat i
Cesarius vnd and martrer vrsprung geno

# The Legend of St. Valentine

Here's a poem about St. Valentine and how he sent a dove to carry the very first valentine. You can make the dove out of paper and decorate it with watercolors. Then write the poem on the back, if you like.

## HERE'S WHAT YOU WILL NEED★

8½″ × 11″ piece of watercolor paper, or other heavy, rough, paper
watercolors, brushes
pencil, tracing paper, carbon paper
black fine-line marker

## HERE'S HOW TO DO IT★

**1.** Following the directions given on page 9, trace the illustration onto the watercolor paper. Go over all of the design with the black fine-line marker.

**2.** Using the watercolors, paint the dove whatever colors you would like. It is going to be a very fanciful bird, so don't be afraid to use plenty of bright colors.

## THE LEGEND OF ST. VALENTINE★

*Centuries ago, an evil king imprisoned a friendly priest named*
*Valentine.*
*Under a churchyard garden, full of flowers that bloom in the sun*
*He was made to live in a dark prison cell.*
*Children came to play and sing and amuse themselves in the garden.*
*The children's laughter gave gentle Valentine pleasure.*
*One day a small white dove flew onto his windowsill.*
*He gave the dove a letter to deliver to the children.*
*Then every day he would send a message to his friends.*
*And today these same thoughts are found in valentines!★*

First code

| A | B | C | D | E | F | G | H | I | J | K |
|---|---|---|---|---|---|---|---|---|---|---|
| Z | O | X | B | D | G | J | K | C | L | N |

| L | M | N | O | P | Q | R | S | T | U |
|---|---|---|---|---|---|---|---|---|---|
| Y | P | Q | E | S | T | F | A | U | I |

| V | W | X | Y | Z |
|---|---|---|---|---|
| M | V | R | W | H |

Second code

| A | B | C | D | E | F | G | H | I | J | K |
|---|---|---|---|---|---|---|---|---|---|---|
| 10 | 3 | 8 | 7 | 88 | 9 | 5 | 1 | 2 | 13 | 16 |

| L | M | N | O | P | Q | R | S | T | U |
|---|---|---|---|---|---|---|---|---|---|
| 6 | 55 | 45 | 33 | 12 | 23 | 17 | 18 | 20 | 17 |

| V | W | X | Y | Z |
|---|---|---|---|---|
| 73 | 22 | 21 | 4 | 66 |

# Secret Codes and Invisible Writing

A walnut shell is a great object to hide a secret message in. Open the nutshell carefully, so that each half is perfect. Eat the walnut if you like! Now make your secret message.

A good spy has a great deal of imagination and a very good memory. Here are three codes for you to try. Write them down on a small piece of paper so that you can use them easily. You can share the codes with a friend and send messages to each other. (Remember to store the codes in a safe place after you've finished using them.)

The first code is an easy one. All you do is substitute another letter for each letter of the alphabet. In the second code, numbers are substituted for each letter of the alphabet. And in the third one, a simple design substitutes for each letter of the alphabet.

Invisible writing is another method for sending secret messages. Milk works best for writing invisible messages, with a toothpick for the pen. After writing your secret message, how do you read it? All you, or the person you are writing to, have to do is heat the paper. Carefully hold the message up near a light bulb. Keep moving the paper until the entire message appears. Magically, it will appear right before your very eyes.

**HERE'S WHAT YOU WILL NEED★**

walnut, pen or pencil, writing paper, milk, toothpick, lamp

Third code

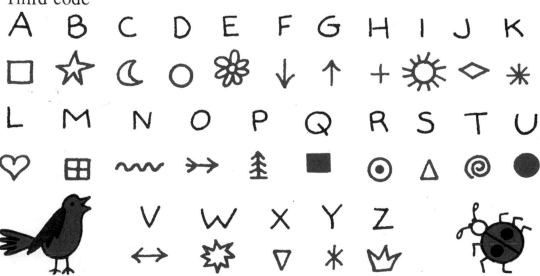

# "Lucky" Rag Doll

This is a good luck charm that carries the spirit of St. Valentine. The doll wears a button necklace, has a red heart, and carries a heart. You can make a boy, Valentine, or a girl, Valerie.

## HERE'S WHAT YOU WILL NEED★

8½″ × 11″ piece of muslin, or other solid-color
   fabric for the doll's body
scissors, string
scrap of printed fabric for Valerie's belt
black fine-line marker
pink colored pencil, red marker
scraps of yarn, white glue for the hair
needle, thread, and 20 buttons for the necklace
scrap of white oaktag for the heart

## HERE'S HOW TO DO IT★

**1.** To make the doll's head, chest, and legs, take the piece of muslin and cut off a piece that is 6″ × 11″. Along the 11″ side, fold the fabric in half and then in half again. Now press down on the folds with your hand.

**2.** To make the hands and arms, take the remaining piece of muslin and cut it to 5″. It will be 5″ × 2½″. Along the 5″ side, fold it in half and then in half again.

**3.** Take the first piece of fabric and fold it in half so it measures 5½″ high. You are going to make the head by tying a string to secure the neck about 1½″ from where it is folded, as shown in the illustration. Now tie some string around the waist. Insert the arms between the neck and waist. To make the hands, tie some string around each lower arm. Finally, separate the leg pieces, as shown.

**4.** For Valerie, tie some printed fabric around her waist for a belt.

**5.** To make the face on your doll, first look at the illustration and then experiment on a piece of scrap paper. With the black marker, draw the face onto the doll. Using the pink-colored pencil, make circular shapes on the doll's cheeks to give it a rosy face. With the red marker, draw a heart onto the doll, as shown. Use the scraps of yarn to make some hair for your doll. Check the illustrations for some ideas. You can make braids, curls, a ponytail, or even a spiked hairstyle. Just glue the yarn on the doll's head.

**6.** For the necklace, pull the thread through the buttonholes and then tie it around the doll's neck. Finally, cut out a small heart from the oaktag, make a small hole at the top and pull a thread through it, and then tie it to the doll's hand, as shown in the drawing. Your tiny companion is now complete.★

# Sun/Moon/Star/Heart Valentine

Don't miss a chance to give your valentine the sun, moon, a star, and a heart! All you have to do is cut them out and string them on a piece of red ribbon and you're all set.

**HERE'S WHAT YOU WILL NEED★**

white oaktag
pencil, scissors
hole punch, red ribbon, red marker

**HERE'S HOW TO DO IT★**

**1.** These shapes are so simple that you can just draw them lightly onto the oaktag with the pencil and cut them out.

**2.** Punch a hole in the center top of each piece, as shown. Put the ribbon through the hole and tie it with a knot. If you like, you can write a little message on the heart with a red marker.★

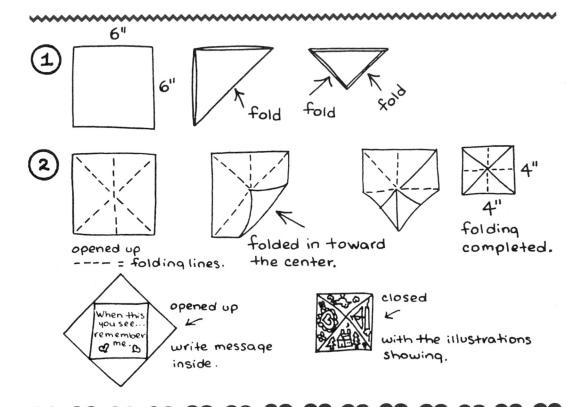

① 6"

6"

fold    fold    fold

② opened up
- - - - = folding lines.

folded in toward the center.

4"

4"

folding completed.

When this you see... remember me.

opened up
write message inside.

closed
with the illustrations showing.

# Puzzle Pocket Valentine

This is another old-fashioned valentine from about the middle of the 1800s. A piece of paper is folded to form a pocket. The outside has a drawing on it and the inside has a message.

## HERE'S WHAT YOU WILL NEED★

6″ square piece of white paper
pencil
tracing paper
tape
colored pencils or markers

## HERE'S HOW TO DO IT★

**1.** Begin by folding the piece of paper in half, along the diagonal, then in half again, and then in half again, as shown in the illustration.

**2.** Open up the paper and flatten it out. Now fold each of the corners in toward the center, as shown. When you finish doing this, you will have a 4″ piece of paper that is your puzzle pocket. Inside, write a message that might have been written on the long-ago originals— "When this you see . . . remember me"—or anything else that you like. Copy the illustrations on the outside, following the directions given on page 9, and then color them in.★

FOLD

# Classic Super Special "V"-Type Racing Cars

You can make a couple of these "V"-type racing cars and have a special Valentine's Day race. Put a different number on each car and away you go!

**HERE'S WHAT YOU WILL NEED★**

7″ × 5″ oaktag for each car
tracing paper, pencil
black fine-line marker
colored markers, scissors, tape
a penny for each car
masking tape

**HERE'S HOW TO DO IT★**

**1.** Following the directions given on page 9, copy the pattern for the racing car.

**2.** Fold the oaktag in half along the long side. Draw the car onto the oaktag. Draw over the lines with the black marker. Color in the car and give it a number, checking the illustrations for ideas. Cut out the car.

**3.** Put a piece of tape over the penny and tape it inside the back end of the car. This will give the car a little weight, enabling it to race better.

**4.** Make as many cars as you have players and decide on how far you want to race. A good distance is about eight feet. Make a starting line by putting down a piece of masking tape on the floor. Arrange the cars just behind it. Next make your finishing line with tape, about eight feet away. To race your cars, get down on the floor and blow at the rear of your car. This will make the car go. The first car to cross the finish line is the winner.★

# Have a Heart Pin

This sweet-looking heart is covered with buttons and can be an instant family treasure. Check your family's button box and pick out your favorite ones. They can be from your old clothes, your mother's blouses, your father's old shirts, your sister's or brother's or even grandparent's clothes.

## HERE'S WHAT YOU WILL NEED★

scrap of cardboard
pencil, scissors
white glue
25 assorted buttons, up to an inch across. Buttons
    with flat backs are the easiest to use.
safety pin, tape

## HERE'S HOW TO DO IT★

**1.** With the pencil, draw a heart shape no bigger than a real heart on the cardboard, as shown. Cut it out.

**2.** Beginning along the outside edge of the heart, glue the buttons onto the cardboard. When you get to the center, you can overlap the buttons if you need to.

**3.** Glue the safety pin to the back of the cardboard heart and then cover it over with a piece of tape. While you wear your button heart, think of all the memories that are attached to each of the buttons you used.★

M & the will shine forever

# Valentine Rebus

A rebus is a word-picture puzzle. It is an amusing way to write out a valentine message, using simple words and some pictures.

The message is "Be my valentine and the sun will shine forever dear!" Now, try to make up a rebus of your own.★

## HERE'S WHAT YOU WILL NEED★

8½″ × 11″ piece of white paper, envelope
pencil
tracing paper
black fine-line marker
colored felt-tip markers, colored pencils, or watercolors
paintbrushes

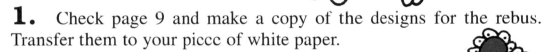

## HERE'S HOW TO DO IT★

**1.** Check page 9 and make a copy of the designs for the rebus. Transfer them to your piccc of white paper.

**2.** Go over the pencil lines with the black marker.

**3.** Use either the markers or watercolors to color in the designs. Have fun experimenting with different colors and try adding a decorative border, as shown. If you like, you can also make some of these designs on the envelope.

# 3-D Valentine Cards — Owl, Dragon, Cat, Cupid, and Teddy Bear

Designs are given for an owl, a dragon, a cat, a winged cupid, and a teddy bear. All four designs are special because they are 3-D, or three-dimensional. Each has a small piece of sponge glued onto it that stands out.

## HERE'S WHAT YOU WILL NEED (FOR EACH DESIGN)★

8½" × 11" piece of oaktag, folded in half
    along the long side
½" piece of sponge
red felt for the heart
pencil, tracing paper
colored pencils, glue

## HERE'S HOW TO DO IT★

**1.** Follow these basic directions for making each of the designs. Check page 9 and make a copy of the design that you are going to use on your piece of oaktag.

**2.** Using the colored pencils, decorate the card as shown in the illustration. Cut out a heart from the red felt. Glue the piece of sponge onto the design, as shown. Next, glue the heart onto the sponge. This will give a 3-D effect and should look festive and pretty. Try making all of the cards and give them to your friends.★

# Heart Necklace

Twenty-four paper clips bent into heart shapes and locked together form this clever necklace.

**HERE'S WHAT YOU WILL NEED★**

24 paper clips

**HERE'S HOW TO DO IT★**

**1.** Begin by gently and carefully opening up one of the paper clips, pulling each side apart, as shown, to reveal a heart shape. Overlap the two ends slightly to complete the heart.

**2.** After you have shaped the first one, repeat for the other paper clips. Interlock each one as you go along, as shown. Twenty-four paper clips make a nice long necklace. You might like to make one for your mother, grandmother, or special friend.★

# Hearts All in a Row Game

Here is an ancient game for two players that has been enjoyed for centuries, but we can add a new twist. It is played here with tiny paper hearts that you can make and carry around in an envelope.

## HERE'S WHAT YOU WILL NEED★

red construction paper
pencil, scissors
envelope

## HERE'S HOW TO DO IT★

Cut out 32 hearts from the red construction paper. Make them about an inch high. You may follow the directions given on page 9.

To play the game, lay out the hearts in a rectangle or square, as shown in the illustration. In turn, each of the two players takes any number of hearts that are next to each other from any row or column. For example, if the first player takes the top three hearts from the second column, the second player cannot take the whole first row at one time because there is a gap in it. However, he or she could pick up the entire fourth row, because it has no gap, or any number of consecutive hearts on the broken rows. The player to pick up the last heart is the winner.★

# Cupid's Delight Scones

Quick to make as a cupid's arrow—these scones are a little like muffins. They are wonderful with a glass of milk for a Valentine's Day treat.

## INGREDIENTS★

2 cups all-purpose flour
$\frac{1}{2}$ cup firmly packed brown sugar
$\frac{1}{3}$ cup cocoa powder
2 teaspoons baking powder
$\frac{1}{4}$ teaspoon salt
6 tablespoons sweet butter, softened
1 egg
$\frac{1}{2}$ cup milk
1 teaspoon vanilla
2 milk chocolate bars with fruits and nuts
   (5 ounces each), cut into small pieces
confectioner's sugar

## UTENSILS★

measuring cups and spoons
large mixing bowl
small mixing bowl
mixing spoon
pot holders
toothpick
cookie sheet
aluminum foil

## HERE'S HOW TO DO IT★

**1.** **Ask an adult to help you turn on the oven.** Preheat it to 350° F. Cover the cookie sheet with aluminum foil.

**2.** In the large mixing bowl, stir together the flour, brown sugar, cocoa, baking powder, and salt.

**3.** Add the butter and stir until the mixture looks like crumbs.

**4.** In the small bowl, beat the egg, milk, and vanilla together. Add this to the flour mixture and then stir in the pieces of chocolate bars.

**5.** Using the ¼-cup measuring cup, scoop up some dough and drop it onto the cookie sheet. Leave about an inch between each scone.

**6.** Bake for about 15 to 20 minutes, or until a toothpick inserted in the center of a scone comes out clean. Dust with confectioner's sugar and serve warm. Makes about 10 scones. ★

# Red Raspberry Thumbprint Cookies

Send some of these delicious treats to someone special. These cookies store and pack well and are an excellent treat to bring to a school celebration.

## INGREDIENTS★

½ cup sweet butter, softened
¼ cup sugar
1 large egg yolk
1 teaspoon vanilla
1½ cups all-purpose flour
1 cup red raspberry jam

## UTENSILS★

measuring cups and spoons
large mixing bowl
mixing spoon
pot holders
cookie sheets
aluminum foil

## HERE'S HOW TO DO IT★

**1.** **Ask an adult to turn on the oven and preheat it to 350°.** Cover the cookie sheets with aluminum foil.

**2.** In the large mixing bowl, combine the butter and sugar. Beat until light and fluffy. Add the egg yolk and vanilla. Stir until completely combined. Add the flour, continuing to stir until blended.

**3.** To make the cookies, pinch off a small piece of dough about the size of a quarter. Make sure that your hands are clean before you begin this.

**4.** Roll the piece of dough into a ball between the palms of your hands, then put it on the cookie sheet. Lightly press your thumb in the ball's center, leaving a small indentation. Repeat to make the rest of the cookies, placing them about an inch apart on the cookie sheet.

**5.** Using the ½-teaspoon measuring spoon, fill the indentation in each cookie with the raspberry jam.

**6.** Place the cookie sheets in the oven and bake for about 10 minutes, or until the edges of the cookies are slightly browned. Makes about 40 cookies.★

# Sweetheart Fudge

This is a great gift to share with a sweetheart or special friend.

## INGREDIENTS★

12-ounce package of semi-sweet chocolate chips
1 cup marshmallow cream
1 teaspoon vanilla
pinch of salt
1 tablespoon sweet butter, softened
2 cups sugar
¾ cup evaporated milk
extra butter to grease the pan

## UTENSILS★

9″ square baking pan
measuring cups and spoons
large mixing bowl
mixing spoon
medium-sized saucepan
plastic wrap or waxed paper

## HERE'S HOW TO DO IT★

**1.** Grease the pan with the extra butter. Put aside. Ask an adult to help you when you are ready to use the stove. In the large mixing bowl, combine the chocolate chips, marshmallow cream, vanilla, and salt. Put aside.

**2.** **Ask an adult to help you with the cooking now.** Put the butter, sugar, and milk in the saucepan. Place over a low heat on the stove. Stir the mixture until it is well combined. Continue stirring until the mixture comes to a boil and the sugar is dissolved. Allow the mixture to boil slowly for 5 minutes. Remove the saucepan from the stove.

**3.** Pour this mixture over the chocolate mixture. Stir until the chocolate melts and it is smooth. Spread the mixture into the prepared pan. Place the pan in the refrigerator until the fudge is firm, after about an hour. Cut into 1½″ squares. Wrap each piece in plastic wrap or waxed paper and store in an airtight container. Makes 36 pieces. ★

# Chocolate Kiss Oatmeal Cookies

This combination of a chocolate kiss on top of an oatmeal cookie will delight anyone on Valentine's Day or any other day. Try it and you'll see.

## INGREDIENTS★

1¼ cups sweet butter, softened
1¼ cups firmly packed brown sugar
1 egg
1 tablespoon vanilla
1½ cups all-purpose flour
1 teaspoon baking soda
½ teaspoon salt
1 teaspoon cinnamon
3 cups quick or "old fashioned" uncooked oatmeal
16-ounce package of chocolate kisses

## UTENSILS★

measuring cups and spoons
large mixing bowl
mixing spoon
pot holders
cookie sheets
aluminum foil

## HERE'S HOW TO DO IT★

**1.** **Ask an adult to help you turn on the oven and preheat it to 350°.** Cover the cookie sheets with aluminum foil.

**2.** In the large mixing bowl, combine the butter and sugar. Add the egg and vanilla. Beat until the mixture is light and fluffy.

**3.** Add the flour, baking soda, salt, and cinnamon. Stir until completely combined. Stir in the oatmeal until well mixed.

**4.** Drop the batter by rounded tablespoons onto the cookie sheets. Leave about an inch between cookies because they will spread while baking. Place a chocolate kiss in the center of each cookie. Bake for about 10 minutes, or until the edges of the cookies are very slightly browned. Makes about 4½ dozen cookies.★

# Cherry Cheesecake Cupcakes

These delectable little red valentine treats are super-easy to make and will disappear quickly.

## INGREDIENTS★

8-ounce package of cream cheese
1 egg
¾ cup sugar
1 teaspoon lemon juice
1 teaspoon vanilla
1 can of cherry pie filling
12 vanilla wafers

## UTENSILS★

measuring cups and spoons
large mixing bowl
mixing spoon
cupcake tins
12 paper cupcake baking cups
pot holders

## HERE'S HOW TO DO IT★

**1.** **Ask an adult to help you turn on the oven.** Preheat the oven to 350°. Place the twelve paper baking cups in the cupcake tins.

**2.** Mix the cream cheese, egg, sugar, lemon juice, and vanilla together in the large mixing bowl.

**3.** Place a vanilla wafer in each of the paper cupcake baking cups. Then fill each one three-quarters full with the mixture. Bake for 15 minutes.

**4.** Put one heaping tablespoon of cherry pie filling on top of each of the baked cupcakes. Place in the refrigerator for half an hour to cool. Makes 12 cupcakes.★

# Index